D0426117

$4.00

The Prospect
Relationship Ladder™

The Little Book of BIG Secrets for
Getting More Appointments

by Robert E. Krumroy

These strategies positively influenced our production by moving us from an activity driven platform to a marketing platform. This book will dynamically impact your sales. It did ours!

> \- Thomas C. Powers, CFP, ChFC, CMFC, CLU,
> Managing Principal, Waddell & Reed

A GREAT read for anyone in financial sales who wants more appointments and more sales!

> \- Charles E. McDaniels, CLU, ChFC, Principal Financial Group

From the authority on "branding" in the 21st Century, this book is INDIS-PENSABLE. These are the core skills found in high achievers. Don't let them be a secret!

> \- Mark Hillman, Ph.D., Award Winning Author,
> *My Therapist is Making Me Nuts!* seen on CNN, NBC, and Court TV

Performance and retention is directly linked to prospect access. Here's the secret of what must be done to achieve welcomed prospect access in today's market.

> \- Ron Willingham, Author of *The Ten Laws of Wealth & Abundance,*
> *The Inner Game of Selling,* and *Integrity Selling for The 21st Century*

Krumroy stands at the top of the ladder for practical and actionable client acquisition ideas.

> \- Jeff Hughes, GAMA International CEO

Krumroy demystifies today's market skepticism and provides rock solid solutions to gaining an almost unfair competitive advantage in client acquisition. Don't let the competition read this book before you do!

> \- Gerald C. Case, Director, Community Bank of Florida

This is Krumroy at his best. Prospect attraction and client loyalty is determined by feelings, not logic. Read this book and watch your sales and your referrals soar.

> \- Renata Marie Vestevich, national speaker and author,
> *Grant Me My Final Wish*

The Prospect Relationship Ladder™

The Little Book of BIG Secrets for
Getting More Appointments

Robert E. Krumroy

Author of
Identity Branding – Creating Prospect Attraction
Brilliant Strategies and Fatal Blunders
Please…Make ME a little bit FAMOUS!
and
It's NOT About Luck!

The Prospect Relationship Ladder™: *The Little Book of BIG Secrets for Getting More Appointments*

I-B Publishing, Greensboro, NC
ISBN 10: 0-9678661-6-2
ISBN 13: 978-0-9678661-6-1

DEDICATION

To Mom.

*Thank you for raising me to
become all that I am,
and even more important …
all that I am not.
I love you.*

Contents

Acknowledgments

Writing a book is a tremendous undertaking. The work is not about putting down on paper what you want to say. The work involves formulating the thoughts, getting supporting documentation, doing research to quantify the theory and, sometimes, just brainstorming with others who share in your dream of contributing something to the world that will touch thousands of lives. For all of those contributions, my sincere thanks to the entire team at Identity Branding who provide encouragement and input, as well as customer support, on a daily basis.

I particularly would like to thank Brad Whitmore. Not only is Brad an invaluable partner, but a great workshop facilitator and brilliant IT project manager at the same time – a combination that is rare and enviable.

I also want to thank Alan Polczynski. Alan is the best vice president of training I can imagine and also a fantastic group instructor, with an energy level I only had when I was 10.

It is with tremendous appreciation that I give credit to Vanya Reed and Rob Reinbold, who orchestrate our customer support with an unbending commitment to excellence.

To Renee Baber, who negotiates, plans and coordinates all of my speaking engagements.

To Ruby Robinson, who manages finances, books and all of the tedious financial issues I am so bad at.

To LaDonna Bushnell, who works with compliance and legal, keeping me insulated from the insane rules and regulations imposed on this industry. You will be made an angel in heaven someday.

And finally, my thanks to Michelle Polczynski, vice president of operations, who is my voice of reason, a light in the dark, a stabilizing factor that keeps my feet on solid ground (usually) and someone whom everyone likes.

Love and thanks to all for allowing me to be a free spirit in creating and writing, while building a business with the greatest team imaginable.

Preface

Are you ready to eliminate the all-too-frequent "no" to appointment requests? How would you like welcomed access to the majority of prospects you desire to engage? Sound impossible? Wrong. It is possible. There are people who manage to do it every day. Why not you?

Most companies and advisors are obsessed with their product and sales process. There's only one problem: That approach is completely backwards. The focus should be: prospect first, product and process second.

As an advisor in the financial industry, it's all too easy to become hypnotized by company ratings, pricing, national advertising, performance and unique product features. But the fact is, prospect attraction is all about you. It's about ingratiating yourself to your audience by helping them feel good about themselves and emotionally safe when they encounter you.

Top sales pros get it right. They focus on prospect attraction and positioning first, before selling. They sell more, have less anxiety and feel more confident. Their career satisfaction is significantly above the norm. They qualify every year for their company's and their industry's top awards. They are the competition.

How does this quest start? It begins by constructing a **Prospect Relationship Ladder**™ strategy, one that compels your prospects to continue climbing until they reach the top rung: Emotional Safety.

In this book, you will learn what to do, how often to do it, and on whom to focus your attention. But reading it will present a defining crossroad. You will have a choice to make. One choice is to find the book interesting, adopt nothing and continue along in your current state. The other choice is to implement the ideas you find here, make more money, capture a prospect community, gain welcomed access and become your market's competition.

I hope you make the right choice.

Chapter One

Getting the Prospect to Say Yes

"Too many professionals are paying too little
attention to the changing prospect.
This mistake is costing a fortune
in lost appointments and
lost sales opportunities."

What's wrong with the average prospect today? Doesn't he know he should be saying yes to the financial advisor who can reduce his taxes, increase his after-tax wealth, provide better security for the people he loves, and establish better economic strategies for his retirement years?

The truth is, we live in a different world now. Your job no longer begins by figuring out a clever way to slide around a prospect's personal privacy filters in order to get an appointment or finding a clever way to get past the proverbial gatekeeper to his business. Determining in your mind to persevere, relentlessly sell, and push through all the objections is not the way to become a super sales achiever. Becoming louder or more invasive than your competition just doesn't work anymore.

Let's face it. Most prospects consider meeting with the average salesperson to be just another chore – one they aren't particularly fond of accepting in most cases. Even offering to buy lunch doesn't alleviate the average person's anxiety.

The facts speak for themselves. The National Do Not Call Registry, created in 2003 to help people fend off unsolicited pitches, currently contains nearly 150 million home phone numbers. That's between 80 and 90 percent of all prospects! People in general are untrusting, frustrated and tired of coercion in sales or even appointment requests. Every advisor these days has a "getting-in" problem. Prospects, even referrals, are hesitant about saying yes.

The level of skepticism seen in today's market has soared, and it can't be overcome by giving out pens, calendars, baseball caps and water bottles with your logo on them. It is not reduced by having a nice-looking office and reception area (which is expected) or by offering your visitor bottled water (which is nice) or by asking interactive questions during the interview (which is good training, but not unique).

The reality is that today's sale starts before your first encounter. It starts when prospects emotionally conclude they can safely consider meeting with you, before they're even asked.

Constructing a strategy that helps prepare the prospect for an eventual appointment request is imperative if you want to achieve high-level success. To solve your getting-in problem, you must apply a getting-in solution. This is probably not at all what you were taught by your company or sales training department. But it's the bottom line.

Chapter Two

Changing the Prospect's Reaction

"Our primary job is not to relentlessly sell, nor to coerce. It's to draw prospects to the conclusion that they can safely accept an appointment with us."

Consider the fact that every prospect reacts psychologically to an appointment request in one of three ways: fear, indifference or welcomed acceptance.

FEAR

Prospects who don't know you, or know very little about you, very likely will have emotional qualms about meeting with you. This is normal. After all, a cold call by its very nature implies that you want to sell me something. Therefore, the appointment request is not for my benefit, it is for your benefit. It is no mystery that in today's world, most of us naturally defend against cold calls.

Think about your personal cell phone. When it rings, you look at the screen to identify the caller. If you don't know who it is, you don't answer. You let the caller leave a message. The reason: fear. You don't want to fend off intrusive sales calls, solicitations or special offers. It's self protection. You want control – control over whom you are willing to talk with and whom you will allow to monopolize your valuable time.

Even if you're lucky in reaching that cold prospect and you're convincing enough to get the prospect to accept an appointment, the meeting very often will be canceled. If not, you will meet with someone who is emotionally defensive and guarded. Not an ideal situation for maximizing your sales efforts.

INDIFFERENCE

Prospects who know you casually, but not well enough to conclude that you are distinctly different in your field or personally remarkable, may agree to an appointment out of friendship or obligation – but it won't be out of enthusiasm. These friends and acquaintances are indifferent. Many wish they could have said no, but regrettably said yes out of politeness.

I recall in years past agreeing to meet with a church friend about health supplement products. Approached while picking up my daughter after her Sunday school class, I said yes only to avoid offending a friend. It certainly wasn't out of enthusiasm or welcomed acceptance. While driving home, I had this conversation with my wife.

Me: "Guess what, honey? We have an appointment with Fred about his health supplement products Thursday evening. He says he has to do so many interviews each week for his company and he wanted to meet with us."

Wife: "Why did you agree to meet with him?"

Me: "Fred asked for the appointment while I was picking up our daughter."

Wife: "Why didn't you just say no?"

Me: "I wanted to. I tried. But we see him every

week and he has brought it up so many times. I knew if I said no again, it would really offend him. But gee whiz, giving up my Thursday night to talk about vitamins and feeling obligated to buy something is the last thing I want to do. I like Fred. Maybe if we're lucky, he'll have to cancel."

Wife: "Probably not. It's a better chance that we will just have to pretend we're enjoying the encounter and then figure out how to get him to leave without offending him."

Now that's indifference!

Imagine that conversation occurring after you convinced one of your hesitant friends or acquaintances to accept an appointment. If they have no pre-established validation that tells them (with no uncertainty) that you are remarkably different and more market-attractive than the other financial person they have done business with in the past, they're going to be indifferent about meeting with you – at best. They may be hoping you have to cancel. That's a bad foundation for beginning an interview.

WELCOMED ACCEPTANCE

Prospects enthusiastically and without hesitation accept appointment requests from individuals they deem to be emotionally safe. Usually we consider parents, brothers, sisters, longtime friends and those who have extended themselves personally to us in relevant and caring ways to be emotionally safe. These are people we trust to have our best interests at heart. We may additionally consider a minister or psychologist to be emotionally safe because they have proven to be trustworthy. But we don't place people in the emotionally safe category just because they are excellent in their line of work. Excellence may be a prerequisite to getting the sale, but it is not the reason someone accepts that first appointment.

Chapter Three

Building Emotional Safety

"Sporadic initiatives don't create reliable trust.
Your share of local market
personal visibility and likability is
more important than your company's share
of national name recognition."

Prospect attraction is no longer primarily the result of your company's name recognition, your product, your sales training or your degree of proficiency in your field. It is far more dependent on a strategy that connects and keeps connecting you to prospective clients in ways that make you likable, trusted, personally distinct and… finally… emotionally safe.

Emotional safety is created through one or more of these three methods:

- Repetitive and relevant exposure that is eventually considered remarkable
- The discovery of a shared cause, values or friends
- An encounter with you that delivers a surprising act of personal kindness

To illustrate this point, here is the Prospect Relationship Ladder. Observe that most training causes advisors to approach prospects with an appointment request while they're in the beginning Superficial Connection Steps. They have not progressed up to the Bonding Steps. It's no wonder advisors get discouraged about their appointment success.

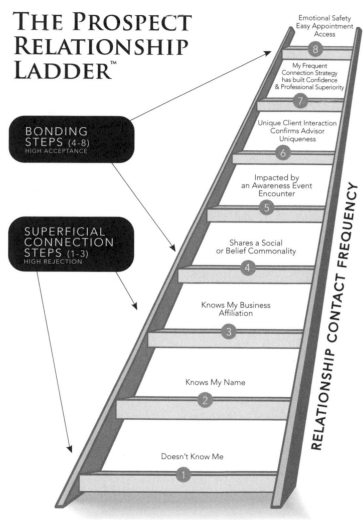

The Prospect Relationship Ladder™

BONDING STEPS (4-8)
HIGH ACCEPTANCE

SUPERFICIAL CONNECTION STEPS (1-3)
HIGH REJECTION

RELATIONSHIP CONTACT FREQUENCY

8 — Emotional Safety Easy Appointment Access

7 — My Frequent Connection Strategy has built Confidence & Professional Superiority

6 — Unique Client Interaction Confirms Advisor Uniqueness

5 — Impacted by an Awareness Event Encounter

4 — Shares a Social or Belief Commonality

3 — Knows My Business Affiliation

2 — Knows My Name

1 — Doesn't Know Me

A description of each ladder rung is depicted below.

LADDER RUNG #1

Doesn't Know Me

Contacting a prospect at this level is termed "cold" and usually not welcomed. The agent making a cold call is likely to be as anxious as the person he's approaching. Cold calling was effective in the 1970s. It isn't today. People guard against being contacted by those they don't know. Approaching someone who doesn't know you is proof positive you're trying to sell him something. He considers your appointment request to be all about you, not about him. Keep climbing the Prospect Relationship Ladder and watch your results continue to improve.

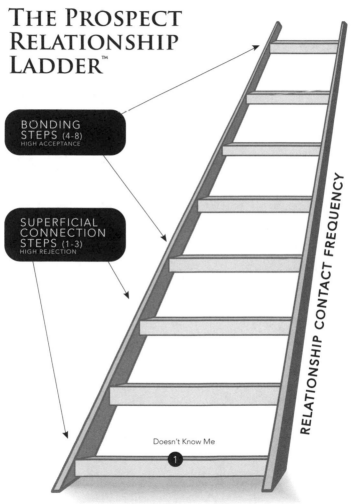

THE PROSPECT RELATIONSHIP LADDER™

BONDING STEPS (4-8)
HIGH ACCEPTANCE

SUPERFICIAL CONNECTION STEPS (1-3)
HIGH REJECTION

RELATIONSHIP CONTACT FREQUENCY

Doesn't Know Me

1

27

LADDER RUNG #2

Knows My Name

Does this sound familiar? You meet someone new at a social function and determine, as a salesperson, to follow up with a call a few days later. Much to your surprise, that pleasant social encounter didn't extend itself to business. The response may not have been rude, but it was not successful. No is no, regardless of how it is expressed. This rung of the ladder is a Superficial Connection Step, not a Bonding Step. Keep climbing the Prospect Relationship Ladder and watch your results continue to improve.

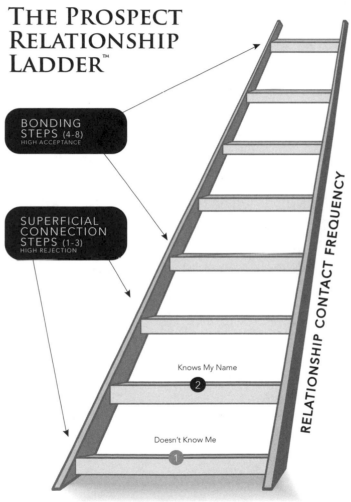

THE PROSPECT RELATIONSHIP LADDER™

BONDING STEPS (4-8)
HIGH ACCEPTANCE

SUPERFICIAL CONNECTION STEPS (1-3)
HIGH REJECTION

Knows My Name
2

Doesn't Know Me
1

RELATIONSHIP CONTACT FREQUENCY

LADDER RUNG #3

Knows My Business Affiliation

Casual acquaintances may appear to be likely candidates for appointments, but often this doesn't prove to be the case. When our knowledge of a prospect is limited to her name and what she does for a living, a conversation about work may be courteous but has no meaningful connection unless both of you know others in her field. Shallow connections don't help you gain appointments. After all, this rung of the ladder is still a Superficial Connection Step, not a Bonding Step. Keep climbing the Prospect Relationship Ladder and watch your results continue to improve.

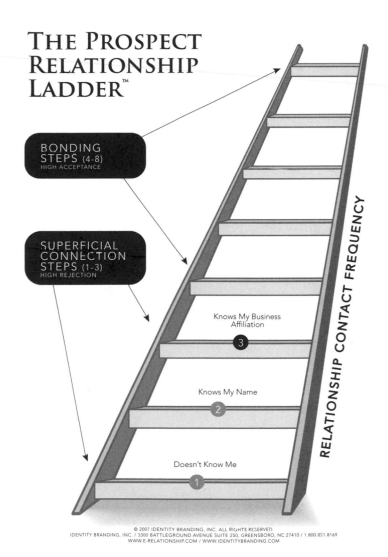

THE PROSPECT RELATIONSHIP LADDER™

BONDING STEPS (4-8)
HIGH ACCEPTANCE

SUPERFICIAL CONNECTION STEPS (1-3)
HIGH REJECTION

Knows My Business Affiliation
3

Knows My Name
2

Doesn't Know Me
1

RELATIONSHIP CONTACT FREQUENCY

LADDER RUNG #4

Shares a Social or Belief Commonality

You are now progressing from the Superficial Connecting Steps and moving upward onto the Bonding Steps. Let me explain why that is important.

When advisors remain dependent on calling cold or barely lukewarm prospects in the Superficial Connection Steps, the continual rejection will eventually kill their motivation. The end result is an advisor who resigns in order to pursue another career path or a mediocre-producing senior advisor who stays put, never attaining significant prospect influence within a specific market.

High-level producers climb the Bonding Steps, building a visible presence in a specific, identified prospect market. The result is a career that is both financially and emotionally fulfilling.

THE PROSPECT RELATIONSHIP LADDER™

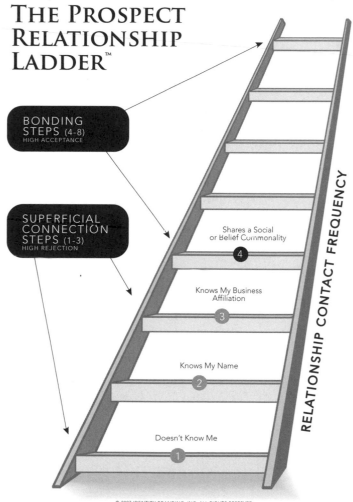

BONDING
STEPS (4-8)
HIGH ACCEPTANCE

SUPERFICIAL
CONNECTION
STEPS (1-3)
HIGH REJECTION

Shares a Social
or Belief Commonality
4

Knows My Business
Affiliation
3

Knows My Name
2

Doesn't Know Me
1

RELATIONSHIP CONTACT FREQUENCY

33

The Bonding Steps usually begin when both parties identify a commonality – whether it's based on friendships, values or beliefs. Depending on the intensity of the commonality link, trust between the two parties may actually soar, moving your relationship directly to the emotional safety zone.

Deep trust often automatically occurs when individuals discover their commonality is a profound religious belief, a dual language culture or involvement in a deeply personal social cause. Comparatively, getting involved in a professional, civic or occupational association won't create as intense an emotional link. However, it still moves you significantly upward into a bonding phase with fellow members. The impact of getting involved in an occupational association should be a serious component of every advisor's business strategy. There is no substitute for the advantage you gain. Don't procrastinate. Get involved in an association that meets regularly and watch your results continue to improve as you climb farther up the Prospect Relationship

Ladder.

Here are a few occupational associations to investigate. Select one to visit during a monthly luncheon meeting and then commit to getting involved: homebuilders, HVAC, electrical, rubber and plastic mold injection (average business owner income exceeds $350,000), restaurant, manufacturing, landscaping, plumbing, HR association (these members control all company benefits, have access to owners and have tremendous influence on 401k rollovers for retiring employees), and women business owners (NAWBO). Not enough to spur your interest? Google "associations – (your city name)" and consider targeting one or two of the hundreds that will appear. There is no excuse for not getting involved. Join something and then don't be an "empty chair." An empty chair renders no attraction. Build your presence in an occupational association and watch your production soar.

LADDER RUNG #5

Impacted by an Awareness Event Encounter

We often forget that agents, not corporate name recognition, create the conditions for brand acceptance. Brands are created when prospects determine that the experience (YOU) is more memorable and relevant than the competition. The consumer's experience with YOU is the brand. You – not your company or your firm – are in charge of building a compelling attraction. It is your job to position yourself publicly in experiences that are so relevant and memorable that prospects are compelled to talk about you. You are now moving rapidly up the Bonding Steps of the Prospect Relationship Ladder where appointments will become readily accepted or, at worst, politely deferred with an agreement to call back at a later date.

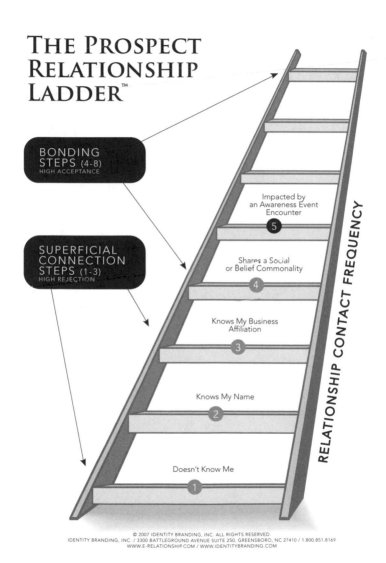

THE PROSPECT RELATIONSHIP LADDER™

BONDING STEPS (4-8)
HIGH ACCEPTANCE

SUPERFICIAL CONNECTION STEPS (1-3)
HIGH REJECTION

Impacted by an Awareness Event Encounter
5

Shares a Social or Belief Commonality
4

Knows My Business Affiliation
3

Knows My Name
2

Doesn't Know Me
1

RELATIONSHIP CONTACT FREQUENCY

LADDER RUNG #6

Unique Client Interaction Confirms Advisor Uniqueness

Never underestimate the power of surprise. When clients encounter a surprising experience, one they feel is unique to how you treat clients, you have given them something to talk about. If you assure them that their referrals will be delivered the same experience, giving names becomes personally advantageous, elevating their prestige with their peers. So give your clients something to talk about. Surprise your Top 20 clients with an ongoing yearly experience that keeps them marveling at your uniqueness, compared to what they believe is the norm in your industry.

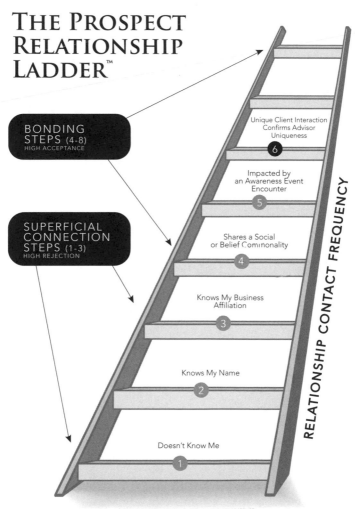

THE PROSPECT RELATIONSHIP LADDER™

BONDING STEPS (4-8)
HIGH ACCEPTANCE

SUPERFICIAL CONNECTION STEPS (1-3)
HIGH REJECTION

Unique Client Interaction Confirms Advisor Uniqueness
6

Impacted by an Awareness Event Encounter
5

Shares a Social or Belief Commonality
4

Knows My Business Affiliation
3

Knows My Name
2

Doesn't Know Me
1

RELATIONSHIP CONTACT FREQUENCY

LADDER RUNG #7

My Frequent Connection Strategy Has Built Confidence and Professional Superiority

Nothing impacts the Bonding Step more than frequent connection. Occasional visibility, such as sending a greeting card sporadically or running into prospects in the community, does not build confident trust. To build the highest level of trust with your prospects, visibility must be frequently consistent (usually requiring a well thought out strategy), assuring them that you are distinctly different, more client focused and more dependable than the competition. When that occurs, you create confidence and assurance. Consistent visibility is the hallmark of prospect attraction. There is no substitute. This is the most important rung in the Prospect Relationship Ladder for creating emotional safety.

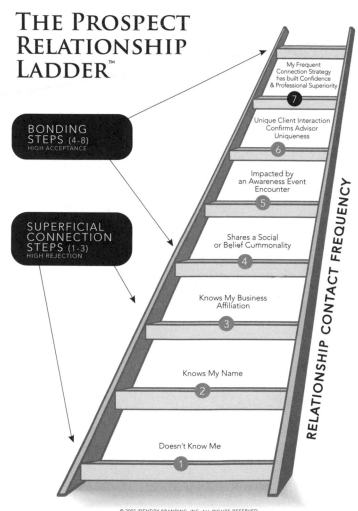

THE PROSPECT RELATIONSHIP LADDER™

BONDING STEPS (4-8)
HIGH ACCEPTANCE

SUPERFICIAL CONNECTION STEPS (1-3)
HIGH REJECTION

7 — My Frequent Connection Strategy has built Confidence & Professional Superiority

6 — Unique Client Interaction Confirms Advisor Uniqueness

5 — Impacted by an Awareness Event Encounter

4 — Shares a Social or Belief Commonality

3 — Knows My Business Affiliation

2 — Knows My Name

1 — Doesn't Know Me

RELATIONSHIP CONTACT FREQUENCY

TOP LADDER RUNG #8

Emotional Safety

As you continue to climb the Bonding Steps with your prospects, your efforts are always well rewarded. It is the most effective means of constructing a bridge to a community where the majority of prospects will welcome your appointment requests. At this level, your reputation as a salesperson changes to that of valued professional. You are considered emotionally safe. Fear of meeting with you is gone. Your intentions are trusted, your opinion is valued and your recommendations are embraced.

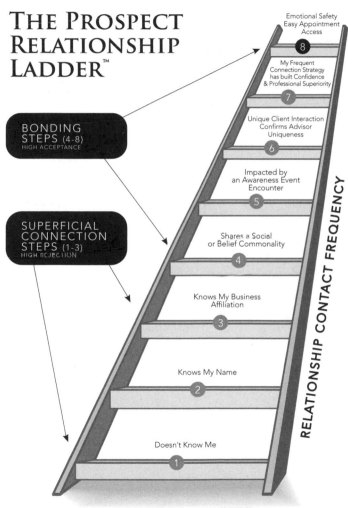

THE PROSPECT RELATIONSHIP LADDER™

Emotional Safety
Easy Appointment
Access

8

My Frequent
Connection Strategy
has built Confidence
& Professional Superiority

7

Unique Client Interaction
Confirms Advisor
Uniqueness

6

Impacted by
an Awareness Event
Encounter

5

BONDING
STEPS (4-8)
HIGH ACCEPTANCE

Shares a Social
or Belief Commonality

4

SUPERFICIAL
CONNECTION
STEPS (1-3)
HIGH REJECTION

Knows My Business
Affiliation

3

Knows My Name

2

Doesn't Know Me

1

RELATIONSHIP CONTACT FREQUENCY

THE FOUR CRITICAL STEPS

Appointment acceptance and personal fulfillment increase when you take the time to build a prospect-attraction strategy, allowing your prospects to climb the Prospect Relationship Ladder by encompassing these four critical steps:

1. **Build a significant prospect database** (at least 1,000) by identifying groups of people you would like to make up the lion's share of your business. Make sure you legitimately enjoy the prospect clusters you choose to target. Most successful prospect clusters are a combination of religious, social and occupational targets. Rarely can you ignore joining at least one occupational cluster in order to build quantity and visibly shine with your prospects. Consider your local homebuilders association, landscapers association, HR association (they control all benefits and access to the owner), National Association of Women

Business Owners, veterinary association, etc. Add these names to your database and then continually add the names of new people you would like to have as clients. Your prospect database should always be increasing in order to stay current with your increasing talent level.

2. **Once a year, formulate a number of strategic actions** that will deliver you in a highly visible, consistent and personal way (not business!) to your prospect database. Sporadic initiatives don't work. They won't create emotional safety. Neither will they create reliable trust. Build a consistent touch-point strategy that is highly visible.

3. **Embrace visible actions** that will consistently deliver your business uniqueness to your clients – especially to your Top 20.

4. **Make consistent contact** 15 to 18 times a year with your entire prospect and client database. Consistent visibility builds trust

and confidence. There is no substitute for this.

Once you embrace the objective of moving your prospects up the Prospect Relationship Ladder to the Bonding Steps, you will quickly begin building emotional safety and prospects will respond more positively to your appointment requests.

The average person is deeply anxious about meeting with the typical salesperson, perhaps more than you imagine. Consider that a survey conducted by ComScore Networks (comscore.com) in 2006 found that 61 percent of respondents would be willing to slightly lower their standard of living if they could live in a world devoid of advertising. Yes. Devoid of advertising! People are untrusting and aggravated by everyone trying to get into their pockets - especially those with whom they have no knowledge or trust.

It should be no surprise that an occasional

encounter with a new prospect at a chamber of commerce luncheon no longer provides enough positive impact to gain an appointment. Even engaging in a little luncheon chit-chat usually won't help. People you don't know well want emotional safety first and foremost, rather than an explanation of what you do.

What makes you more widely appreciated within your prospect community or with the people you meet at the chamber of commerce? What builds admiration for you and leaves the competition in the dust?

When you can answer those questions with confidence, using the four strategic components that help your prospects climb the Prospect Relationship Ladder, you are on the way to becoming a super achiever.

"Agreeing that local marketing is a good idea
won't increase your production.
The journey begins by embracing a new and
repetitive action that is going to be seen
by your prospects as
surprisingly remarkable,
uniquely relevant and personally beneficial."

When you do the same thing everyone else does, your potential is limited to never exceeding the norm. Even if your product beats the competition, there is still no compelling reason for your client to talk to others about you or to give you referrals.

Good products are expected. They aren't the foundation for making clients share your story with their friends. Even so, most financial companies keep trying to rally salespeople around competitive comparisons of their product or sales process. Instead, they should be rallying them around their prospects.

We forget that financial companies don't make brands; they make products and services. People, not companies, create brand acceptance. Brands are created when people determine that the local experience is relevant. YOU are the brand.

In a nutshell, when prospects have a personal experience that is out of the norm, one they consider uniquely relevant, surprising and personally valuable, prospect attraction is born. The agent – the experience giver – is now considered emotionally safe. The prospect feels obligated to respond to an act of kindness with an equal act of kindness. Agreeing to an appointment is an easy payback.

Since you, the agent, are in charge of building a compelling attraction, it is your job to set the conditions necessary for the prospect to enthusiastically climb the Prospect Relationship Ladder. It is your job to create experiences that are unique and so enjoyable that your prospects are compelled to investigate and conclude that you are emotionally safe.

Here is an example of an attraction event, focused on attracting veterinarians and their clients to you. Twenty additional ideas are in the marketing kit described in the back of this book. There is an idea for everyone. Find something you like and implement it.

THE VETERINARIAN CONNECTION

An estimated sixty-three percent of American households have pets – that's more than 71 million homes. No longer just furry creatures roaming around the house, they've become valued family members, incurring a larger share of our spending than any other interest or outside hobby. Veterinarians, as a result, are practically members of the family as well.

It's easy to see why veterinarians make potentially great clients. They're highly respected. They make an excellent income and have plenty of job security. Their clients trust and love them. They have the ability to deliver you to a significant quantity of great referrals.

Achieving preference with these professionals is not about name recognition or proclaiming your expertise. It's about evolving their personal feelings, causing a positive emotional connection to you.

Feelings of trust and affection don't happen in

one encounter. They accumulate over time. Build your strategy and allow the feeling of connection to evolve. Here are your four objectives:

1. **Locate veterinarians** within your community. Veterinary medical associations are an easy place to begin. If you intend to focus on the entire local veterinarian market as an occupational association, join the veterinary association as an associate member, attend the monthly meetings, get involved, and build your visibility. To find information about your local association, go to an online search engine such as www.google.com and plug in the association, your city and state. If your area doesn't have an active veterinary association, you can use the yellow pages or recommendations from friends. Focus on 20 to 30 veterinarians.

2. **Insert the veterinarians' names into e-Relationship.** This will be your initial method for introducing yourself and then

consistently accentuating the financial areas in which you specialize. It is also your system for sending yearly e-holiday cards and three special cards created just for your veterinarian prospects:

- World Veterinary Day *(last Saturday in April)*
- National Dog Day *(August 26)*
- National Cat Day *(October 16)*

3. **Set a strategy** (see idea below) with two to four select veterinarians to ingratiate you in a very special way through a series of unique, relevant and surprising encounters.

4. **Create an opportunity** with your select veterinarians that will attract their clientele. Conducting a Pet Tag and Child ID Day (see details below) will provide an exceptionally surprising and delightful encounter with their clients. The veterinarian will be rewarded by gaining new patients and increasing the appreciation of existing ones. You will be rewarded by the large

numbers of the veterinarians' clients you will meet.

Here is the special yearly connection strategy for your select two to four veterinarians:

- Insert these dates in your calendar: the last Saturday of April (World Veterinary Day), August 26 (National Dog Day), and October 16 (National Cat Day).

- Make arrangements for the following items you will deliver to the veterinarians' offices: a box of cupcakes on World Veterinary Day, a biscuit platter on National Dog Day, a bagel platter on National Cat Day.

- Don't delegate the delivery of the food. You need to be visible to achieve impact. Clear your schedule, deliver the food and have fun.

- Have a pre-printed note displayed on each platter, along with your paper-clipped business card. Here are examples of these notes:

World Veterinary Day
(Last Saturday in April – _deliver the food on Friday_)

Tomorrow is World Veterinary Day. It was founded in 2001 to recognize the highly respected and compassionate veterinarian profession. As a financial professional who focuses my practice on a few special occupational groups (one of them being veterinarians), I want to thank you for the good things you do for many of my clients and their pets. Again, my thanks for your contribution to our community and to the animals in our lives.

Sincerely,
(Name)
(Phone Number)

National Dog Day
(August 26)

We love our dogs. They are unselfish, patient, grateful, friendly, forgiving and loyal – quite possibly the nearest to perfection of all living things. Today, on National Dog Day, it's appropriate that we take the opportunity to say "Thank You!" to those in the veterinary profession who take care of them. With much gratitude to you and your office, hopefully this biscuit platter expresses my thanks for all the value you deliver to our community *(or substitute "to us dog lovers")*. Additionally, if I can ever provide you with information on financial issues, please give me a call. Working with veterinarians is my specialty and it is always good hearing from my veterinarian clients and friends.

Sincerely,
(Name)
(Phone Number)

National Cat Day
(October 16)

Cats have so many personalities, but all offer companionship and unconditional love – something we cherish more the older we get. Mark Twain said, *"Of all God's creatures, there is only one that cannot be made slave of the leash. That one is the cat. If man could be crossed with the cat it would improve the man, but it would deteriorate the cat."*

Today is National Cat Day, a day to say "Thank You!" to the veterinarians who take care of our cats. So with much gratitude, hopefully this bagel platter expresses my thanks to you and your office for the value you deliver to our beloved pets and their families. Additionally, if I can ever provide you with information on financial issues, please give me a call. Working with veterinarians is my specialty and it is always good hearing from my veterinarian clients and friends.

Sincerely,
(Name)
(Phone Number)

Once you have accumulated a list of veterinarians you would like to influence, put their names into your e-Relationship account and send e-messages and e-holiday cards throughout the year. People conclude that the person they see the most in any category of business is the highest-level expert. Let the veterinarians see you more frequently than anyone else and watch the opportunities for business open.

Be patient. The cumulative effect of your connection efforts will pay off over the course of a year. Don't prematurely stop your veterinarian connection strategy and neglect to deliver the food platters three times each year. Once you have established a friendship, it is now time to approach the veterinarians about a yearly joint venture involving their clients.

E-Photo Album Tip to Maximize the Event's Impact

Have a digital camera on hand to take photos of the attendees with their pets and children. After the event is over, assemble the pictures into the e-Photo Album and send it to the attendees. Seven days later, send an e-Financial Storyboard and enjoy the tremendous quantity of responses. After meeting you and experiencing a surprising and relevant encounter, these prospects will welcome your approach. This is how relationships are started and how they evolve.

Email to Attendees after the Event

Subject Line: Pet Tag (and Child ID) Day Follow-Up Message

Thanks for stopping by our Pet Tag Day. It is always nice to see friends and meet new people who share the same deep affection for their pets as I do for mine. I will make sure

The Pet Tag and Child ID Day

Hold this event on one of the following dates:

- National Flea Day *(the Saturday between June 25 and July 1)*
- Walk the Dog Day *(February 22)*
- Adopt-a-Dog Month *(October)*
- Do Something Nice Day *(October 5)*

Suggest to your veterinarian that you would like to co-sponsor a combo event – a free Pet Tag and Child ID Day – as an appreciation event for both the veterinarian's clients and your clients. If you hold this on National Flea Day, the veterinarian may have access to free samples of flea repellent to give to attendees. If the veterinarian's practice is extremely large, holding this event at the clinic may attract a large crowd. But usually you will want to hold it at a PetCo Store, a PetSmart store or some other pet supplies store in a desirable shopping area. Getting permission from the retailer should be simple.

The objective of this event is to deliver a memorable experience, paving the way to easy that we contact you next year when we repeat this event.

I may have mentioned that my regular business specialty is working with families on financial issues. In regard to that, I am including some financial tips and information in the following link. If it triggers your interest, feel free to request the additional details at the end. I'll send you a new tip or update every few months. In the meantime, love your pet! They always return the affection.

[e-Financial Storyboard here]

Sincerely,
(Your Name)

Never underestimate the power of surprise. Identify connection opportunities with prospect clusters you would like to attract. Deliver compelling experiences. Embrace surprise! We loved surprises when we were kids and we still love them today.

Pleasurable, surprising events provide the foundation for prospects to consider you emotionally safe. The result will be an increase in first-time appointments, numerous new referrals and a reputation that will position you as superior to the competition.

Chapter Five

Impacting Your Referral Success

"Humans by nature are storytellers.
We enthusiastically engage in communication
and referral-giving when we believe it increases
our level of prestige or affirms our status
among peers. If you want your clients to
enthusiastically give referrals,
give them something to talk about."

At the end of a sale, it's good traditional advice to review the benefits your client has accomplished before asking for referrals. However, there is a secret that can catapult your referral results to new heights.

When a client is surprised by an unexpected act of kindness, one he assumes is your unique way of doing business, referring you to others becomes a benefit to him versus a benefit to you.

When you surprise a client with an unexpected act of kindness not related to your product or process, it increases her confidence that she is doing business with "the best." It also provides a "moment of influence," a fleeting moment in time when the client feels obligated to return the kindness.

Never miss the opportunity to ask for referrals during moments of influence. The word "moment" is not synonymous with "sometime in the future." When a moment of influence occurs, the time to act is now.

When clients feel confident that their friends will experience the same surprise and delight (above and beyond the product or process), referring you to a friend is a way for them to emotionally elevate their personal prestige. When the referral process is seen to benefit them, you have positioned yourself to attain your greatest results.

Elevating our position with friends is psychologically the greatest reason we volunteer information when we talk. When we pass on non-vital information that begins with "Did you know…" or "Did you hear…," it's an unconscious hierarchical attempt to affirm our status. Even negative gossip serves to elevate our positioning. It's just the way we are as humans.

Therefore, when recommending a friend, we are most enthusiastic when we believe the experience that the referral will receive will affirm or elevate our status. The surprising experience is more important than the product or even the sales process when determining if we should refer a friend. It's what provides the emotional impact.

How do you accomplish the goal of having clients see referral-giving as a personal benefit to them?

First, pose these questions to yourself:

What special experience do you provide to your most valuable clients that is personal – having nothing to do with the product, your consultative fact-finding or the sales process? What personal thing do you do that makes them conclude you are extraordinarily superior to the competition?

What causes your clients to brag to their friends that you are the best?

What do you do that makes you more widely appreciated than the product?

What do you do that delivers proof positive to clients that you are different and more deserving than any other advisor within your community?

When your sales process is finished, do your clients feel emotionally compelled to enthusiastically refer you?

There are numerous ideas employed by high-achieving sales professionals in today's market. The difference between average producers and high achievers is that high achievers consistently implement their attraction strategies – strategies they have spent time constructing. They pick one meaningful idea and implement it consistently, without fail, every single time. It eventually defines them in the market.

Here is a brief overview of a few strategies that can be used at the end of a sale to increase referrals and build your reputation for being distinctly superior relative to the competition. These strategies remove the focus from the financial action and return the client to the personal and emotional. The prospect has already reciprocated on your financial work by purchasing your recommendation. However, he has not reciprocated on this special action, giving you a new "moment of power" in which to ask for and receive referrals. (Full details of each strategy can be found in the marketing kit at the end of this book.)

1. At the end of the sale, give a copy of *Grant Me My Final Wish* by author Renata Marie Vestevich. This impressive journal (beautiful inside and out, with a soft padded cover) is written as a way to build a family legacy. Its thirteen sections include places to preserve family memories, insert photos and write messages conveying words of love and values for future generations to read. This journal affirms that you genuinely care about your client in a very personal way, not just financially. With this gift in your client's hand, now is the perfect time to ask for referrals while assuring him that the referrals will also receive copies of the

journal. *Grant Me My Final Wish* regularly sells for $24.95 but can be purchased in quantity for between $12.50 - $15 at www.bellavitabooks.com, or call (800) 589-0039.

2. Deliver a cake to your Top 20 or Top 40 clients on their birthday every year. Don't be embarrassed. There is no more thoughtful gesture, no greater surprise. Time the delivery for 11 a.m. The referrals will flow if you and your client then break away for lunch. Your client will brag to the referrals before you can even call them, often causing them to comment about how much their friend enjoyed the surprise. After all, you gave them something to talk about.

3. Buy new clients or your Top 20 or Top 40 clients a subscription to *Islands* magazine. (Do not substitute a business magazine. They are not regarded as a personal.) The cost for an *Islands* magazine annual gift offer (shelf price is $78 for the year) is only

$14 and is delivered eight times a year, making it a gift that's hard to forget – particularly when your name is included on the address label. You can order gift subscriptions to include your name, listed as "compliments of" on the label under the recipient's name. Putting a simple instruction on the order form will accomplish this. (An order form is in our marketing kit.) If this is a new sale, show the client the magazine and you will create a new moment of influence while asking for referrals. For existing clients (or Top 20), send letters alerting them to the subscription and explaining it is your way of showing appreciation for their business. Call them within 60 days to verify that the first issue has arrived, listen to their thank-you, and invite them to lunch. The referrals will flow. After all, you gave them something to talk about.

4. Keep a case of special wine or fancy sparkling Italian lemonade and orangeade by Le Village (available by the case at

Amazon.com for $6 a bottle) in your office. When the sale is complete, excuse yourself for a minute and return with a bottle or two wrapped in a box or tied with a bow, and a note welcoming them as a special client. You may mention that you deliver a bottle of wine every holiday season to your best clients or that you hold a wine tasting every year for your clients and that they will certainly be invited. Now ask for referrals and observe the higher level of enthusiasm you just created.

When clients and prospects position you above the average me-too financial professional, they see you as emotionally safe – someone who is genuinely concerned about them, not just their financials.

Give your clients something to talk about. Do something that is totally unexpected. Trump the competition with a personal act of kindness and watch your confidence and your referral results soar.

Addendum

Taking it to the Next Level

"Competitive products are no longer unique;
advanced support is not a differentiator;
hope is not a strategy.
Take a day to build an attraction strategy,
be consistent in implementation, and watch
your reputation soar above the norm."

In today's ever-changing world, it is the wise business person who dares to open his mind to new ways of capturing clients and outperforming the competition. Congratulations! In reading this book, you have made a solid investment in a brilliant future.

You are off to a good start. And now that you know the basics, you're ready to learn more about how to refocus and energize your efforts. Allow me to introduce you to a powerful set of programs and tools created by Identity Branding that will give you the inspiration, motivation and skills to be consistently successful.

The Prospect Attraction Workshop

In this concise and lively program, we teach you how to create a market attraction strategy that elevates your personal visibility, professional image, confidence and prospect approachability. The workshop is available in either a three-hour or five-hour format and includes a 14-page workbook for each participant. The agenda includes:

- History – What has changed in the market-place?

- Attraction – The six new psychological rules of client and prospect attraction.

- Prospect clusters – Are you engaged in a defined occupational, civic or affinity target market but still have problems getting welcomed appointments? Not all markets are equal. They require different strategies to build welcomed access. Learn what markets have the greatest potential and discover the most effective ways to approach them.

- Activating events – Ideas and visibility strategies to create local market intrigue, making you famous within your local prospect community.

- Characteristic uniqueness – What are you

doing that creates identifiable uniqueness in your client's mind, making you appear as extraordinarily superior to the competition? The answer is not in your product or your sales process. The skill creates a "moment of power," causing a compelling sense of obligation where the client willingly responds with meaningful referrals – not just at the end of the sale but continuously through the life of the relationship.

- Staying in touch – Out of sight, out of mind. How true that is! Keeping connected with clients and prospects is the hallmark of prospect attraction and deep client loyalty. There is no substitute. Most advisors miss easy sales due to lack of frequent and relevant connection. Learn what your clients want, what prospects want, and how often.

Please...Make ME a little bit FAMOUS!
Complete Marketing Kit, $99.95

Robert Krumroy's acclaimed financial industry book *Please...Make ME a little bit FAMOUS!* is now available on CD, with 21 mini-marketing booklets as a bonus. This marketing kit is a must-have if you want to build dominant recognition in your local community. Each booklet reveals an awareness strategy used by super achievers to build recognition, surprise, delight and increase appreciation with prospects and clients. Just choose or adapt the strategy that fits your personality and market. All of the information you need to implement a strategy (including sample letters and order forms) is included here. It's an unbeatable way to learn how to open doors in your market.

e-Relationship

The number-one connection tool in the financial industry!

Consistent connection is one of the mainstays of being a highly successful financial advisor. Our e-Relationship automated email software makes it delightfully easy to keep in touch with every prospect and client in your database. Send e-holiday cards, e-birthday wishes, e-newsletters and more throughout the year. Also choose from over 75 prepackaged e-financial information modules. Each message is personalized and sent one at a time – no multiple-name mailing list is ever seen by your recipients.

> One-time activation fee: $99 - $149
> Monthly subscription cost: $59.95 - $79.95
> Pricing depends on your company co-op program.
> Call for your company's pricing.

Index

About the Author

Robert E. Krumroy, known as "The Prospect Attraction Coach," is president and CEO of Identity Branding, Inc. He is also founder and creator of the e-mail marketing tools www.e-relationship.com, www.agent-recruiting.com and www.my-ecustomer.com. Identity Branding is dedicated to helping financial sales professionals create a visibly distinct and unique local market presence, a perception of superior value– eventually creating an almost unfair competitive advantage for themselves. Once accomplished, these professionals can thrive, successfully attracting prospects and outclassing the competition.

With twenty-five years of experience in the financial services industry, the author qualified sixteen times as a National Management Award winner and built his financial service firm into one of the one hundred largest in the country. ***The Prospect Relationship Ladder*** is his sixth book. Previous titles by the author include *Identity Branding – Creating Prospect Attraction, Identity Branding – Revisited, Brilliant Strategies and Fatal Blunders, Please... Make ME a little bit FAMOUS!,* and *It's NOT About Luck!* He has also authored hundreds of columns and magazine articles.

He has served on national teaching faculties and is a highly sought-after speaker, giving more than one hundred clinics and speeches each year to some of the largest companies both in the United States and internationally. He has been introduced often as one of the best marketing minds in the country.